D1366392

Annie Mae's Movement

Annie Mae's Movement

Yvette Nolan

Playwrights Canada Press
Toronto • Canada

Annie Mae's Movement © Copyright 1998 Yvette Nolan

Playwrights Canada Press
The Canadian Drama Publisher
215 Spadina Ave., Suite 230, Toronto, Ontario, Canada, M5T 2C7
phone 416.703.0013 fax 416.408.3402
ders@playwrightscanada.com • www.playwrightscanada.com

publisher acknowledges the support of the Canadian taxpayers through the
nment of Canada Book Publishing Industry Development Program, the Canada
or the Arts, the Ontario Arts Council, and the Ontario Media Development
Corporation.

Front cover image by Leon Aureus.
Production Editor/Cover design: JLArt

Library and Archives Canada Cataloguing in Publication

Nolan, Yvette

Annie Mae's movement / Yvette Nolan.
A play.
Originally published: Toronto : PUC Play Service, 1999.

ISBN 0-88754-904-7

Aquash, Anna Mae, 1945-1976--Drama. 2. American Indian
Movement--Drama. I. Title.

PS8577.O426A65 2006   C812'.54   C2006-903388-9

First Playwrights Canada Press edition September 2006
Second printing June 2009
Printed and bound by Canadian Printco at Scarborough, Canada

"A nation is not defeated until the hearts
of its women are on the ground."
—Cheyenne saying

for all the brave-hearted women

Annie Mae's Movement was first presented as a staged reading at Native Earth Performing Arts' Weesageechak Begins to Dance Festival of new plays, Toronto, Ontario, in February 1998, with the following company:

Anna Mae Aquash   Rose Stella
Rugaru/Lawrence/Dennis/
Doug/FBI Guy/Law   Tom Hauff

Directed by Anne Anglin

• • •

A workshop production of this revised version of *Annie Mae's Movement* was produced by Native Earth Performing Arts, in March 2006 at the Factory Studio Theatre, Toronto, Ontario, with the following company:

Anna Mae Aquash   Michelle St. John
Rugaru/Lawrence/Nogeeshik/
Dennis/Doug/FBI Guy/Law   Ryan Cunningham

Director: Yvette Nolan
Dramaturg: Sarah Stanley
Set Design: Christine Plunkett
Lighting Design: Michelle Ramsay
Sound Design: Richard Lee
Ghost Shirt: Louis Ogemah
Production Manager: Stephen Lalande
Stage Manager: Isaac Thomas
Oompah Loompah: Nina Lee Aquino

The premiere of *Annie Mae's Movement* was produced by Hardly Art, Whitehorse, Yukon, in September 1998 with the following company:

Anna Mae Aquash   Sophie Merasty
Rugaru/Lawrence/Dennis/
Doug/FBI Guy/Law   Archer Pechawis

Director: Yvette Nolan
Assistant Director/Dramaturg: Valerie Shantz
Set Design: Don Watt
Lighting Design: Scott Boone
Music: Jay Burr
Vocals: Jerry Alfred
Ghost Shirt/Image Design: Louis Ogemah
Stage Manager: Jen Jones
Assistant Stage Manager: Lindsay Rawluk
Producer: Kathleen Curtis
Media Coordinator: Angela Heck

The same production, presented by Hardly Art and Red Roots Theatre, ran at the Gas Station Theatre, Winnipeg, Manitoba, in September/October 1998. It was also produced as a part of Eastern Front Theatre's On The Waterfront Festival, Halifax, Nova Scotia, in May 1999.

Characters

Anna Mae Aquash
Rugaru
Lawrence
Dennis
Doug
FBI Guy
Law

Acknowledgements

Philip Adams, Anne Anglin, Brandon University, Canada Council for the Arts, Kathleen Curtis, Angela Heck, DD Kugler, Manitoba Arts Council, Monica Marx, Tracey McCorrister, Native Earth Performing Arts, Louis Ogemah, Valerie Shantz, Sarah Stanley, Helen Thundercloud, Minnie Two Shoes.

Annie Mae's Movement

Beginning

Lights up to reveal ANNA MAE, curled in a foetal position CS. The red silk/red road flows downstage, the good red road. ANNA awakens, begins to crawl, then to walk the road.

ANNA   There are all kinds of ways of getting rid of people. In Central America they disappeared people. Just came and took them away in the middle of the night, whoosh gone, and then deny everything. Very effective. Well, here they disappear people too. They disappear them by keeping them underfed, keeping them poor, prone to sickness and disease. They disappear them into jails. In jails they disappear their dignity, their pride. They disappear our kids, scoop 'em up, adopt 'em out, they never see their families again.

Our leaders—the leaders of the American Indian Movement—said that we should learn to fight. And because we'd never get enough firearms, we had to use the only thing that they couldn't take away from us. We had to train our bodies, turn our hands into weapons. Alright, I said, right on, and I got up at dawn to train with the rest of them. Well, they didn't mean me, did they? They meant the men, the warriors, the dog soldiers. Not you, girl, fighting's not for you. But my first husband, Jake, he ran a martial arts school…

I guess I got it from my mother, she used to fight with the Indian Agent. This one time, he brought us a bunch of clothes, *donations*—army coats and what do you call those pants they wear riding horses?—all motheaten, full of holes. I couldn't have been more than four, but I remember she sent him packing, with his crummy rags. After that, he finally started sending us better stuff.

"You gotta stand up, Anna Mae, you gotta fight for what's important, no matter who wants to shut you up." We have to fight, even if seems like we're fighting ourselves. Or else we will disappear, just disappear.

It's so easy to disappear people in this country, especially Indian people. Scoop 'em up here, drop 'em off there. Whoosh, gone. Then just deny everything.

Anna Mae? Anna Mae Who? Never heard of her…

Whoosh…

She is gone.

Rugaru

The red road disappears. The landscape appears, and then goes to night. The moon is illuminated. The RUGARU appears in silhouette. He is part man, part creature, big and hairy, obviously not of this world. His movement is like that of a man, but not quite. There is something of the animal about him. Canine. Lupine. Something of the supernatural, the ability to be here, and then suddenly there. As he crosses the moon, he stops, turns his head, scans/ smells the audience. He raises his face to the sky and opens his mouth, but the howl that issues is amplified, effected, not of this world. He exits.

Survival School—Boston, 1973

ANNA is tidying up books and assignments.
LAWRENCE is hanging around. She gets her bag
and starts packing things up, putting on her jacket.
LAWRENCE is still hanging around.

ANNA   What's up, Lawrence?

LAWRENCE shrugs.

Is there something you need?

LAWRENCE shakes his head.

Did you want to talk about your paper? I have it here.
"A Nation Built Upon Sand—How the 'United States of
America' Reneged on the Fort Laramie Treaty of 1868."
I'm impressed, Lawrence, your grasp of the historical—

LAWRENCE   I didn't come to talk about my paper.

ANNA   *(beat)* I know you didn't.

ANNA waits, watching him.

LAWRENCE   The Rugaru's been seen on Pine Ridge.

ANNA   So?

LAWRENCE   Forty people saw it. Forty different people. Different
times. Different places.

ANNA   Did you see it?

LAWRENCE   I was sitting at the bonfire with a few people, and
suddenly there was this smell, rank, foul. And then
I heard him breathing, right here, and I held my
breath, but the sound was still there, wheezing, and
I turned my head really quickly, but it flitted just out
of sight. Rugaru.

ANNA is silent.

It's a sign.

ANNA   It's a *sign. (pause)* Of what?

LAWRENCE	It's a sign that things are gonna change for Indian people.
ANNA	Great.
LAWRENCE	*Don't.* Don't be like that. You're not like that.
ANNA	I'm sorry. It's just, I get frustrated when I see people putting their faith in some outside magic, instead of buckling down and doing the work.
LAWRENCE	You don't believe in the Rugaru?
ANNA	It's not that I don't believe in it—
LAWRENCE	I heard it. I *felt* it.
ANNA	Lots of Indian people have felt it.
LAWRENCE	Have you? Have you seen it?
ANNA	What if I have? What does it mean? That I should quit Survival School, abandon my kids, take off on some crusade? What if it's another Ghost Dance, Lawrence?
LAWRENCE	What if it is? You taught us that the Ghost Dance was a powerful movement, Anna Mae, you said, you said, thousands of Indians joined, they had the government in a panic—
ANNA	—and the government sent in the cavalry and slaughtered our people at Wounded Knee without a fight.
LAWRENCE	Well, this time, instead of Ghost Shirts, we'll have guns.
ANNA	No, no, no, no, no, Lawrence. Look, I know what it's like to want change in a hurry, but things don't change that way, not really. Change comes through work, through systematic community work, through schools like this one, and young people like yourself learning to use libraries and law books and getting jobs—
LAWRENCE	Books and white words! This is how we are going to change?
ANNA	Yes, it is.
LAWRENCE	Trying to change me into *wasicu*.

ANNA	Please Lawrence, don't throw away your education. You're a good student, you're doing well here—
LAWRENCE	It's not that I don't appreciate this school. I do. I flunked out of three high schools before I got here. But knowing how to use a library, how to read their law books, what good is that ever going to do me?
ANNA	You have rights under the law. And if you know them—
LAWRENCE	Anna Mae, no laws apply to Indians. If I get stopped by the cops, if I start quoting the law at them, you think they're gonna say, *ooh here's a smart Indian, we're sorry Mr Harper, here's the phone, go ahead and call your lawyer?* Like hell! They're gonna crack me across the face with the butt of their gun, throw me in the back, drive me to the wrecking yard, handcuff my hands through the window and beat the shit outta me. And if anyone dares say anything, they'll say I was resisting arrest. Ask me how I know that.
	ANNA is silent.
	Ask me how I know that.
ANNA	It's not always going to be like this.
LAWRENCE	How can you say that!?
ANNA	Because—I see—
LAWRENCE	You see what? What do you see?
ANNA	I see—a time when our people will be at the negotiating tables as the heads of our sovereign states. Our leaders will be doctors and lawyers and judges.
LAWRENCE	White ways.
ANNA	Maybe. But they are ways we can use to help our people.
LAWRENCE	And how do we get to the table? Do you see that? Are we invited?
ANNA	Yes. No. *(The vision becomes clearer.)* There will be unrest, resistance.

LAWRENCE	Resistance?
ANNA	I see,—an occupation, a blockade, cars and trees, piled up. Armed men—
LAWRENCE	Armed Indian men?
ANNA	White and Indian, face to face, almost nose to nose. And the women—
LAWRENCE	Armed *women*?
ANNA	No, I don't think so, she is talking, she holds them apart, she stands between them like some avenging angel, and the whole world is watching her—
LAWRENCE	Anna?

ANNA sees LAWRENCE in her vision.

ANNA	Oh—

LAWRENCE looks at her.

LAWRENCE	You see that?
ANNA	Yes.

She looks at him. He exits.

Nogeeshik

ANNA is staggering, fighting.

ANNA Com' awwnn, com'awwn ya pigs, com'awwn. I'll take you, I'll take you all, ya lousy bastards. You can't hurt me anymore, com'awwn!!! Whaddya gonna do? Take away my land?! Take away my language? *(laughs)* What else can you take from me?

> *She grabs a bottle, it is ketchup, pours it on her wrists. Wails, drunk and crushed by the weight of history.*

> *NOGEESHIK enters.*

NOGEESHIK Annie! Annie, Christ. Are you hurt? What the hell happened? Who did this to you? Did—

> *He stops. Lifts her wrist. Sniffs. Licks.*

Christ.

ANNA You left me.

NOGEESHIK I was at a meeting.

ANNA I thought you left me.

NOGEESHIK Anna Mae, this, *(taking her hands as he starts to clean her up)* this is not good.

ANNA It's not real, Nogeeshik.

NOGEESHIK But is it really how you feel?

ANNA Sometimes. Sometimes I do, I've got this pain, deep inside, and I don't know what it's gonna take to make it stop.

NOGEESHIK Anna, I been thinking… I wanna make a change…

ANNA You're leaving me.

NOGEESHIK Jesus, woman are you only about yourself?

> *ANNA is mute.*

I am not leaving you. Unless you want to be left. But I wanna go forward.

ANNA   What does that mean? Go forward? You think
              if I knew how to go forward from this shithole
              I wouldn't? I thought this *was* forward, Nogeeshik,
              off the reserve, to the city, but it's so hard, it's so hard,
              leaving my kids…

NOGEESHIK   I know it is.

ANNA   What kind of a meeting was this?

NOGEESHIK   A life-changing meeting.

ANNA   A Jesus meeting.

              NOGEESHIK laughs.

              Oh thank God.

NOGEESHIK   No Anna, not Jesus. It was an AIM meeting.

ANNA   An AIM meeting? Why didn't you call me?

NOGEESHIK   I tried to find you to come. *(beat)* They said at work
              you went for beer.

ANNA   Well you know where we go.

              NOGEESHIK shrugs.

              What, you didn't want me showing up at an AIM
              meeting with beer on my breath? You hypocrite—

NOGEESHIK   I'm quitting.

ANNA   Drinking? *(pause)* You gonna walk the good red road
              then, Nogeeshik?

NOGEESHIK   It's gotta be better than this.

ANNA   This is not so bad.

NOGEESHIK   This is not so good. *(pause)* They're talking about
              action.

ANNA   Oh that's good, they're *talking* about action, yup, that
              sounds just like those AIM boys alright.

NOGEESHIK   There's all kinds of shit going down on Pine Ridge, lots
              of cops, federals, not just tribal, the people there, they
              want AIM to come in and—

ANNA	You're going to Pine Ridge? Don't leave me—
	She grabs him and he throws her.
NOGEESHIK	Get off me, you stink.
ANNA	And you been dry, what? Twenty-four hours?
NOGEESHIK	Godsakes, woman, I don't understand you! You have every opportunity and you just—
ANNA	I *work*, Nogeeshik, I'm not an artist who can get up at noon and ponder my belly button 'til the muse shits on me and I feel inspired to take up the paintbrush, I go to school and try and hammer some pride into young angry men.
NOGEESHIK	Well that's the blind leading the blind.
ANNA	What are you talking about, I got pride.
NOGEESHIK	Why didn't you take the scholarship at Brandeis, Anna Mae? you're always going on about how we need to acquire the white man's tools to beat him at his own game, but you refused to take that chance—
ANNA	And who woulda paid the bills around here? You?
NOGEESHIK	You coulda been a lawyer, not some small potato survival school teacher.

Archer Pechawis
photo by Philip Adams

ANNA	I needed—action. Yeah, I coulda been a lawyer, but every month I was in there would take me further away from the street, from the people, and who knows what kind of person I woulda been coming out at the other end.
NOGEESHIK	At the meeting tonight, they talked about going in to Wounded Knee, it's gonna happen soon, because things are heating up fast there.
ANNA	I'm tired of marches, Nogeeshik. God, we shout and yell and demand and insist, and all we see in the papers is the uppity Indians are whining again, when are they gonna get over it—*if* we get any coverage at all—
NOGEESHIK	This is gonna be different, they're saying.
ANNA	Oh it'll be different alright, this time we'll be fighting ourselves, Indian against Indian, the white folks don't even have to do it to us anymore, we do it to ourselves.
NOGEESHIK	You want blood, Anna? Real blood? Or do you prefer the kind that comes in a bottle?
ANNA	I don't *want* blood.
NOGEESHIK	Well, there's gonna be blood before this is all over. Come with me.
ANNA	Where?
NOGEESHIK	Wounded Knee?
ANNA	God, don't we ever learn? Not enough that we were slaughtered once at Wounded Knee—
NOGEESHIK	Well, this time we're armed.
ANNA	Armed.
NOGEESHIK	You want action, Anna Mae. Come with me. Let's do something for our people.
ANNA	Do you love me?
NOGEESHIK	Don't you know I do? I put you above all others.
ANNA	Alright then. Back to Wounded Knee.

Wounded Knee—1973

The stage goes to dark, the night sounds grow. The moon is obscured by cloud. The silhouette of a man passes. There is something of the RUGARU about him. ANNA crawls on, with a heavily loaded pack on her back. It is night and she is running supplies into the besieged Wounded Knee.

ANNA   *(whispers)* Nogeeshik! Nogeeshik! Lawrence? Lawrence! Anyone? Damn. Okay, my girl, okay, okay, okay...

She sits up and struggles to pull out a hand drawn map.

(to the sky) I could use some light here.

A flare shoots overhead, illuminating the sky. She hits the dirt, then looks up.

The stage is illuminated by the flare.

Okay, those would be the FBI's over there, thank you boys.

She reads the map by flare light. She stuffs the map back into a pocket and starts to stand.

Another flare goes up. She crouches.

Cowboys.

VOICE   *(off, whispering)* Hey!

ANNA   *(whispering)* Hey! *(puts hands in air)* Don't shoot, don't shoot, it's Anna Mae Pictou, I've brought food and medicine.

She stands and shoulders her pack, begins to exit. DENNIS enters behind her. Lights change.

Anna Meets Dennis

The American Indian Movement Office in St Paul, Minnesota.

DENNIS So you're the little warrior woman I've been hearing about.

ANNA swings down the pack.

ANNA Hi. Anna Mae Pictou—um—I mean, Aquash. I just got married and I'm not used to the name yet.

DENNIS I was at your wedding at Wounded Knee. Not much else to do during an occupation, might as well go to the wedding of the day. Or have one.

ANNA It was important to me, traditional values. I wanted to show the importance of our traditional ways to the protesters.

DENNIS That's a good reason to be married.

ANNA And it was an honour to be married by Nicholas Black Elk.

DENNIS Seize the moment.

ANNA Yes! That's what Nogeeshik and I thought.

DENNIS Ah yeah. Nogeeshik. Painter, or something.

ANNA He's an artist.

DENNIS So it was a statement. Getting married at Wounded Knee.

ANNA Well, we've been together for—you know—quite a while—

Pause.

DENNIS My name is Dennis—

ANNA Oh I know who you are, of course. I'm very honoured to meet you. Actually we've met before, Trail of Broken Treaties in '72. Actually, I was with the Boston Indian

Council, we joined the occupation of the Bureau of Indian Affairs in Washington.

DENNIS   Really? I don't remember, but—

ANNA   Oh, you wouldn't remember me—

**ANNA/
DENNIS**   —there were a lot of people there.

> *They laugh.*

DENNIS   And now you're occupying our national office in St Paul.

ANNA   Ah, it's a friendly takeover.

DENNIS   Sure that's always what they say. Then the next thing you know, they want to change everything, they got a bunch of ideas for improvements, they know how to make things operate smoother.

> *ANNA is silent.*

I hear you got some ideas.

ANNA   A few.

Sophie Merasty
photo by Philip Adams

DENNIS waits.

Well, for instance, the way AIM is working with survival schools is good, but I think we should be thinking more long-term, you know. Like starting to groom young leaders for the movement—

DENNIS   Long term? Long term. What a concept. I worry that we can keep afloat tomorrow, next week, sometimes, on a good day, next month, and you're thinking about the long-term. The movement lives pretty hand-to-mouth, Mrs Aquash. You want to stabilize AIM, think of ways to raise some serious money to fund these initiatives. That's something useful the women can actually do—

ANNA   I think we have to be thinking about moving forward on a bunch of fronts. Yes, money is one, but the way to ensure the health of the Movement is to imagine it beyond tomorrow, next week, next month.

DENNIS   I suppose you've got ideas on how to go about this long-term planning.

ANNA   A few.

DENNIS   Well, I got a few minutes to listen. Come on in to my office and tell me about your long-term planning, Anna Mae Pictou I mean Aquash.

Anna Amongst The Women

St Paul, Minnesota.

ANNA is sewing a ribbon shirt.

ANNA   Funny how I'm always sewing for other people, but I never sewed for my girls. In Boston, I sewed for two years in a factory, boat cushions and toboggan pads. Well, they couldn't've worn those, but in a way, I guess I was sewing for them, 'cause that's how I paid the rent, put food on the table, bought their clothes. Growing girls need a lot of clothes.

I guess it's good that they live with their dad, and his new white wife, in a nice suburban home. Better than on the reserve where everybody's always hungry, there's no jobs, and the alcohol...

At least with their dad in Halifax there's a chance they'll get vegetables and fruit, and not just a steady diet of frybread. White flour, white sugar and lard. White food, making us fat and giving us diabetes.

Still, it'd be nice if I'd sewed for them. Dresses, maybe, matching jumpers. Or navy for Denise, and pale blue, robin's egg, for Deborah.

She completes the shirt she is working on, bites off the thread.

There. I've finally finished.

She attaches a tag to the shirt cuff with a couple of stitches.

It's just too bad they're so damn labour-intensive. Still, the Micmacs' gift to the world.

Okay so it's not a gift. So we're going to charge the *wasicu* thirty bucks a shirt.

DENNIS enters.

DENNIS   What's this? Very nice, Anna Mae. This one for me?

He takes the shirt that ANNA has just finished.

ANNA Not unless you have thirty bucks.

DENNIS Russ is wearing one, says Darlene gave it to him. And Myrtle gave Jimmy one. You should be proud I want to wear yours.

ANNA Nice try, Dennis. And it's not *my* shirt, all the women make them. To "raise some serious money"?

He reads the pamphlet attached to the cuff.

DENNIS *Ribbon shirt—In the early days of colonization, a band of Micmacs accepted a donation of cassocks during a time of need from a small monastery... decorated them with buttons, braid and ribbons...* but it *is* your shirt, Anna Mae, you're the only Micmac I see in these parts. Did you make this story up?

ANNA It's a fundraiser. A fundraiser. You said yourself that we needed to be less dependent on church groups.

DENNIS It's one shirt.

ANNA We're never gonna raise money if we keep giving away our stuff. As it is we're probably in the hole from all the boyfriends and husbands walking around in them.

DENNIS Well, I think it's as important that we raise our profile. These shirts are distinctive. People see them, they see our pride as Indian people.

ANNA And as a proud Ojibway man, you should be happy to set an example for everyone and cough up the thirty bucks.

DENNIS Al*right*, God but you drive a hard bargain, woman.

He takes the shirt and reaches for his wallet.

Oh! I don't have my wallet. I'll have to catch you later.

He turns to go with the shirt, which she grabs back.

ANNA That's okay. You know where to find me. I'll hold this one special for you.

Beat. Then DENNIS laughs.

DENNIS   Fine. Bring it by my office when you're done your little sewing circle.

He exits.

ANNA watches him go.

ANNA   It's only one shirt.

But it *is* your shirt, Anna Mae, you're the only Micmac *(She pronounces it MickMack.)* I see in these parts. Did you make this story up?

I think it's important that we rai-ai-aise our profile— *(She is being rude.)*

ANNA exits.

Archer Pechawis
photo by Philip Adams

Doug

DOUG enters. He is a big man, with a John Wayne walk and attitude. He wears a beaded belt buckle and lots of big turquoise jewellery. He has long black hair, but it is fake, over which he wears a headband in the manner of the other young men of AIM. ANNA enters.

DOUG Hey.

ANNA Oh hi.

ANNA starts to cross past him.

DOUG What's up?

ANNA Oh I just gotta see Dennis about something.

DOUG Nobody gets to Dennis without going through me.

ANNA What?

She laughs and goes to pass him. He blocks her.

You're not serious.

DOUG Dead serious.

ANNA That's pretty serious.

DOUG Dennis and I have decided that we have to institute a new security policy around here.

ANNA Dennis and you, eh? Wow, we're turning into them.

She goes to pass him again. He blocks her again.

DOUG He's busy right now, Anna Mae. Tell me what you need and I'll pass the message along.

ANNA What? Who do you think you are, wannabe?

DOUG I am the new chief of security, Anna Mae.

ANNA Whoohoo! Well congratulations on your promotion.

DOUG And for your information, I am one fourth Ojibway.

ANNA	As my mama used to say, if a man's gotta tell you what he's got, he's already lost it.
DOUG	Oh how quaint, a little Micmac wisdom.
	ANNA shakes her head and starts towards the office. DOUG quickly—too quickly—blocks her way and grabs her. She breaks his hold.
ANNA	Keep your hands off me.
DOUG	Look, Annie, I know it's kinda weird, but we have to take some precautions. Things are heating up for the Movement, the trials are underway. An informer could really hurt the defence team.
ANNA	You gonna ferret out AIM spies for us, Doug?
DOUG	You have to admit I have some experience in these matters.
ANNA	We don't need cops in the Movement.
DOUG	Dennis appreciates the fact that I used to be a cop.
ANNA	Dennis can be—naïve.
DOUG	Look, Annie... I know we got off to a bad start, but I think we should try to get along. I mean, we're on the same side—we want the same things—we were both at the Knee—
ANNA	You were at Wounded Knee for five hours. *(pause)* And you took pictures.

DOUG is silent.

Why are you here, Durham?

DOUG is silent.

Let me by, *wasicu*. I gotta see Dennis.

DOUG blocks her without touching her. She crosses to the phone and hits the intercom.

Hey, Dennis. You got a minute? Just outside your door. Beats me. 'Kay.

She hangs up.

He says come on in.

DOUG steps out of her way. She walks towards the door and stops.

Oh. And Doug? My name is Anna Mae. Anna Mae. Only my friends call me Annie.

She exits.

Dennis And Anna

Late. St Paul.

ANNA
It *is* different for you. Russ says it, Russ says women should know that their roles are different from men's, they shouldn't try to become something they aren't; that there's a natural balance that should be respected, that a good woman is not interested in "taking glory," he says it looking right at me, like I'm in this for glory.

DENNIS enters with takeout food, wearing the ribbon shirt.

DENNIS
Yeah, but Russ thinks he's the reincarnation of Crazy Horse.

ANNA
Your close personal friend Crazy Horse.

DENNIS
To his credit, he didn't think that up himself, someone told a reporter she thought he was, and Russ saw it in print and believed it.

ANNA
I'm not in it for glory, Dennis.

DENNIS
None of us are in it for the glory.

ANNA
What are we in it for? It takes so much, it devours you, this thing. You lose all sense of who you are except in context of the Movement. It's like the Movement becomes the solution for every problem—you're a drunk—AIM doesn't condone drinking—bingo you're not a drunk—you beat your woman—that's not proper for an AIMster, bingo problem gone—your welfare runs out early and you can't afford to eat—hunger is noble in service of the Movement—someone will order in food—takeout!—though your kids may be hungry at home. It's like the Movement has become everything—home, family, social life. We have to renounce everything. It's insatiable.

DENNIS
Why is this a bad thing, Anna Mae? Many of these people had nothing, thought they *were* nothing. We

gave them hope, gave them back their pride in being Indian people.

ANNA But what kind of an organization demands that you give everything up? What are we, Moonies?

DENNIS We are all here of our own free will.

ANNA That's what frightens me. That I willingly leave my girls, willingly give up my children. I tried to keep us together in the beginning. I did. I kept the girls with me when I first came to the States, but what kind of a life is that for kids, dragging them everywhere. Kids need stability, routine. *(pause)* You got kids?

DENNIS Fifteen.

ANNA Fifteen?

DENNIS That I know of.

ANNA Fifteen? You trying to populate the Movement by yourself?

> *DENNIS shrugs.*

You miss them?

> *DENNIS shrugs again.*

Fifteen. God. I miss my two so much. Maybe it's different for mothers.

DENNIS Maybe it is. I don't think of them as my kids—I mean, it's like I think of all Indian kids as my kids—

ANNA Sounds close to the truth—

DENNIS You're shocked.

ANNA Of course not.

DENNIS What then?

ANNA It's just—unfair.

DENNIS That I have fifteen kids?

ANNA That it doesn't seem to phase you. You know, the last time I saw my girls, one of them told me "You know what, Mommy? We'll never forget you, Mommy."

DENNIS	That's a happy thing, isn't it? My kids don't even really know who I am.
ANNA	Why would they be thinking of forgetting me? Then when I left, I found that Jake—that's their father—had stuffed some documents into my jacket saying he had exclusive custody. They knew that I was losing them. That I'd lost them.
DENNIS	This is what we do. We are warriors. We leave the kid raising to others.
ANNA	But raising kids is important.
DENNIS	I'm not saying it isn't. But you are doing other things for your kids, for all Indian kids. You are out there fighting to change the world for your kids. You are a warrior, Anna Mae, and it has a cost.
ANNA	I'm a better warrior than I am a mother, that's for sure.
DENNIS	You're not like any woman I've ever known, I'll give you that.
ANNA	You mean who would leave her kids.
	She moves away from him. He talks to her back.
DENNIS	I mean who I felt was my match, who I depended on so completely, who was my most trusted lieutenant in this struggle.
ANNA	Do you really?
DENNIS	You are so powerful, Annie. I would be afraid of you if I didn't trust you so much. You are a brave-hearted woman.

Anna Writes To Denise

Pine Ridge, South Dakota.

ANNA has a picture of her daughters with her.

ANNA It's better this way, sweetie. It's better you're not here with me. It's too hard, this life, too unsettled.

When you grow up and have your own children, you'll understand why I had to do this, and why I couldn't keep you with me.

At least you'll be able to have children, healthy children, Denise, which is more than I can say for most of the women here. I've never seen so many miscarriages. Barbara just lost her third since I been here—oh I know they say women miscarry all the time and don't even know it, they're pregnant and something goes wrong right away and your body just lets it go, but still, so many—

The RUGARU appears.

Birth defects too. Babies with small heads, little eyes, these jaws. *(motions)* Angela just had a little girl, toes all joined together, but that can be fixed.

Maybe it's the diet, so much crap they eat here, and the women just seem so unwilling to make a change. Or maybe it's all the garbage on the reserve, or there's something in the water…

The RUGARU fades away.

That's the other thing, Denise, you get sick, at least your dad can take you to the doctor, you can get medicine, get taken care of. Here, we're doing bake sales and rummage sales to support a health centre.

You see, sweetie, it's better this way. I am so grateful to the creator that you and your sister are healthy and well cared for—I know you don't understand why I can't be with you right now, but baby—I'm keeping

track of all of this, I write these letters to your Auntie
Becky and when you're older you can read them and
maybe you'll forgive me—

Dennis Sends Anna To Los Angeles

DENNIS enters behind ANNA.

DENNIS   Oh doom-and-gloom Annie Mae. C'mon back to bed.

Grabs her, caresses her.

ANNA   I hate this. I feel like I'm cheating on Kamook.

DENNIS   *I'm* the one who's cheating on Kamook.

ANNA   I know, but she's *my* friend.

DENNIS   She's *my wife. You're* supposed to feel like you're cheating on Nogeeshik.

ANNA   You know my marriage is over.

DENNIS   You're better off without him, Annie.

DENNIS caresses her.

ANNA   I can't help feeling that I'm doomed now, because I've violated the pipe—

DENNIS   You! C'mon, you sweat, you smudge, you walk the walk. How have you violated the pipe?

ANNA   Those traditional vows I took at Wounded Knee, they meant something to me—

DENNIS   Well, that's good, that they meant *something* to you.

ANNA   I think, maybe, I didn't realize at the time what fully... I was—was—

DENNIS   Impetuous?

ANNA   *(beat)* Good one, Dennis. Impetuous. *(beat)* I didn't realize what being married under the pipe meant, and now—I'm bringing some bad shit down on myself for sure.

DENNIS   For God's sake.

ANNA   It's true, Dennis.

DENNIS   This is exactly why I don't follow the traditional spiritual stuff, Anna Mae, why I'm more of a practical,

	political Indian. All this ooga booga shit—you take something practical like a tradition, a ritual and you fill it up with meaning because it satisfies something in you, you give it more meaning than it has. It becomes like "don't play with fire, you'll pee the bed"—
ANNA	What?
DENNIS	As kids, we'd be sitting around poking the fire with sticks, finding things to throw in, see what they did and my kokum would smack us and say "don't play with fire, you'll pee the bed" and sure enough, someone would. It wasn't magic, though it felt like it to us. It was just a practical trick grownups used to keep kids from doing something stupid, and our little kid brains turned it into self-fulfilling prophecy.
ANNA	You think I am wishing bad things on myself.
DENNIS	I think we've got our hands full dealing with the flesh and blood reality of day to day life without blaming it on signs and superstition.
ANNA	Well, if I die under "mysterious circumstances," I want you to—
DENNIS	Annie, they haven't resorted to killing our women yet.
ANNA	*You* were there when they beat Sarah Bad Heart Bull on the Custer courthouse steps—
DENNIS	At the trial of the man who murdered her *son*.
ANNA	Why is it that only men are martyred in this movement?
DENNIS	You want to be a martyr?
ANNA	No, God, no. I want to go home and get my kids from my ex and his new white wife—
DENNIS	Well, that's too bad, because I was gonna ask you to do something.
ANNA	What?
DENNIS	Nope, no, you're going back to Nova Scotia, gonna live a normal life.

ANNA	Tell me, Dennis, come on.
DENNIS	Don't worry, I can ask Doug, he'd be happy to do it.
ANNA	Doug! That weasel.
DENNIS	It's funny that you hate Doug so much, you two are so alike.
ANNA	I am *not* like Doug Durham.
DENNIS	*(shrugs)* Doug is willing to roll up his sleeves and do whatever needs to be done.
ANNA	I do whatever needs to be done.
DENNIS	Doug has a bunch of skills.
ANNA	I have skills.
DENNIS	You're right, you're not at all like Doug.
	ANNA hits him and pulls away.
	(pulling her to him) Well, there is one thing you have to offer that Doug doesn't.
ANNA	Tell me what it is you want me to do.
DENNIS	I was going to ask you—I wanted you—I need you to go to LA and help set up the West Coast office.
ANNA	LA?
DENNIS	I know, but someone has to go, and there's no one better suited to it than you. We need to start bringing in some money, and I think the LA AIM office is going to be the way. Besides, someone has to keep an eye on Doug out there or the whole thing could go sideways—
	She hugs and kisses him.
	So you'll go.
ANNA	Hey. You're not just trying to get rid of me, are you?
DENNIS	Annie.
	He touches her face.
ANNA	Okay. LA. Okay.

Anna And Doug

The LA office. ANNA is working. As she moves within the space we become aware of the lurker on the other side. It could be a man, it feels like the RUGARU. ANNA goes through a bundle of letters, opens one. Looks through them, holds a few of them up. Opens a couple, tosses them aside, opens a third, reads with interest. Exits.

DOUG enters.

DOUG goes through the pile of letters, holding each up to the light. He chooses two and slips them into his pocket. Starts to go through files, drawers.

ANNA enters, holding the letter, watches him.

ANNA Looking for something?

DOUG Annie, hey. I was just…

Pause.

ANNA Just?

DOUG Dennis asked me to send him a list of current donors. I woulda asked you but you seemed busy—

ANNA Dennis did.

DOUG Yeah, he's thinking that if there are some heavy hitters on the LA list, he might be able to get them out to St Paul for a benefit—

ANNA Damn, you're good.

DOUG I told him he should talk to you, that you were the one who talked to the stars, but he seems to think you're too busy with bigger things.

ANNA You know, that's an almost credible story.

DOUG *(shrugs)* Look, pick up the phone and call St Paul, ask him yourself.

ANNA I just got off the phone with St Paul.

DOUG	Oh—good. Dennis?
ANNA	*(holding up a letter)* You know what this is Durham?
DOUG	How would I know what it is, Annie?
ANNA	Well, you go through my mail often enough.
DOUG	Annie—
ANNA	This is a request for a receipt. For a donation—a sizable donation—made to AIM that I never saw.
DOUG	That's weird.
ANNA	Yeah. Weird.
DOUG	So do you think it got lost in the mail?
ANNA	No, Doug, I don't think it got lost in the mail, I think someone has been pocketing donations, donations!—You got some nice little account set up somewhere, Doug? How much have you skimmed off so far? Thousands? Tens of thousands?

Sophie Merasty
photo by Philip Adams

DOUG	This is crazy, Annie—
	She crosses to the bundle of letters, flips through them.
ANNA	Jesus, you already picked through this, didn't you?
	DOUG crosses swiftly behind her, but she turns, feeling him, taking a defensive stance.
DOUG	Look, Annie, call St Paul—
ANNA	They're on their way.
DOUG	Who is? Dennis?
ANNA	Apparently they've been doing a little checking while you've been out here in LA, they wanna talk to you—
DOUG	Annie—
ANNA	It's over Durham, The sneaking around, the drawer rifling, the embezzling—

She gingerly reaches into his pocket and pulls out the two envelopes.

And Durham. It's Anna Mae. Anna. Mae.

She exits.

FBI Guy Outed / Speaking Tour

> *Throughout this, DOUG removes his Indian gear—*
> *choker, rings, headband, contact lenses, hair.*

DOUG   Yeah, I was a full-fledged member of the American Indian Movement since Wounded Knee. I cannot believe how easy it was to infiltrate AIM, I mean these people have no criteria for membership, anyone could join... so I just waltzed in there and became their security chief.

There are those of you who are sitting there shaking your heads, going tsk-tsk-tsk, thinking why does the FBI need to undertake covert operations on citizens of the United States? You want the truth?

You people have no idea.

You think of these people as quaint throwbacks, leftovers from the wild west, from the frontier days. Don't be naïve. What would you say if I told you that AIM is scheming to disrupt our nation's bicentennial celebrations next year? That AIM has training camps around the country in which political indoctrination, marksmanship and guerrilla warfare are taught? That the AIM agenda will lead to the indiscriminate killing of whites? AIM has links to international terrorist organizations, to communist groups.

There are threats to the security of this great nation that cannot be allowed to exist unmonitored. Organizations like the FBI track the activities of subversive groups who present a threat to the state. AIM is not the first group, nor the last, that will be infiltrated and disrupted by the FBI. Would you have let the Black Panthers go? Or King's Southern Christian Leadership Conference? These outlaw organizations with ties to terrorists are a grave danger to the civilized world and will be confronted. There is no bigger task than protecting the homeland of our country.

We have ways of dealing with these groups. Not *outside* the law, but around the edges of it. The good of the many over the good of the few.

Sometimes our covert operations don't work as well as we'd like and we have to try another tack. We thought that Martin Luther King would take care of himself for us, the press was so bad on him, sex scandals and disgruntled blacks, but he was stronger than we thought. His family was strong, his wife—But where one suggestion fails to take root, another will…

In '68, when King was scheduled to go to Memphis, the media received a memo suggesting the good doctor was a hypocrite because he had reservations at the white owned and patronized Holiday Inn, instead of the black owned and run Hotel Lorraine. The fine Hotel Lorraine, the FBI memo called it. Doctor King changed his reservations, moving to the Hotel Lorraine, where he was assassinated in front of his hotel room.

Ironic, isn't it?

Our counterintelligence program is basically very simple: infiltrate, disrupt, sow the seeds of doubt in a few people's minds, they do the rest for you. Pretty soon everyone is pointing the finger at everyone else and the most trusted lieutenant is under suspicion. That's how you bring an organization to its knees.

I'll take a couple of questions now. Uh, *(pointing)* you!

    DOUG exits.

Anna Arrested By FBI—1975

> *Sound of helicopters, searchlights.*
>
> *FBI GUY charges her.*

FBI GUY   You! You! I've been looking for you all over.

> *He handcuffs her.*

ANNA   What's the charge?

FBI GUY   Illegal possession of dynamite.

ANNA   Dynamite?!

> *ANNA sees other FBI GUYS ransacking the Running home.*

Hey! What are they doing? Tell them not to touch those things, those are sacred things!

FBI GUY   Get back over there.

ANNA   Those are not toys, that's Diane Running's medicine—

FBI GUY   You've got more to worry about than a few trinkets.

> *During this, FBI GUY strips her and searches her for whatever.*

ANNA   Those things are sacred. Medicine pouches, eagle feathers, pipes. Do we go into your churches and throw your holy things on the floor? Do we stick your crosses in our hair and dance around?

> *He throws her in a chair. Undoes her handcuffs. Exits.*

The AIM National Convention At Farmington—May 1975

> ANNA waits. DENNIS enters unseen and watches her for a time. She senses him. Turns and stands.

ANNA   Hi.

DENNIS   Hi.

ANNA   God, it's good to see you.

DENNIS   It's been a busy time.

ANNA   Busy.

DENNIS   This convention's taking a lot of manpower. You'd think that after five years it would run itself.

ANNA   I haven't seen you much on Pine Ridge.

DENNIS   Well, the trials, you know…

ANNA   How's Kamook? And your daughter?

DENNIS   They're fine. They—She's very supportive of me, comes to the courthouse in Custer every day, sits where I can see her—

ANNA   Dennis—

DENNIS   I can't, Annie. My marriage to Kamook is important for the Movement…

ANNA   I know that. I'm not asking you to leave her. I just—

DENNIS   I can't. *(pause)*

ANNA   Did you get my letter?

> DENNIS removes it from a pocket.

DENNIS   You can't—it's too risky—don't send me letters, Annie. You know how it is, someone is always opening your mail, they don't always know the difference between personal stuff and AIM business—

> DENNIS extends the letter to her.

ANNA   It's not mine. It's yours. I wrote it to you.

DENNIS	I can't—there's no place in my life that isn't open to examination, Annie.
ANNA	It's just a poem, Dennis.
DENNIS	I—promised—Kamook.
ANNA	Kamook?
DENNIS	I promised Kamook that I would give it back to you. And tell you—
ANNA	Kamook—knows?

DENNIS nods. ANNA groans.

DENNIS	Someone told her about us.
ANNA	Who would—why would—
DENNIS	I don't know. Someone who doesn't like you.
ANNA	Or you.

DENNIS is silent.

What? What else? Dennis?

DENNIS	There's been talk.
ANNA	There's always talk.
DENNIS	We've got some pretty high-placed leaks.
ANNA	Dennis, this is me. Dennis.
DENNIS	We have to be careful now.
ANNA	Of course we do. But we have to be careful that we don't fall into their trap. This is exactly what they want, exactly! All running around pointing fingers at each other, jumping at shadows. They don't have to do anything, they just stand back and let us destroy ourselves.
DENNIS	I don't know who to trust anymore.
ANNA	I told you, I warned you about Doug. If you guys would just listen to the women, it wasn't just me, there wasn't a woman who would turn her back on him—

DENNIS	We can't run a political movement on women's intuition, Anna Mae.
ANNA	I went to hear him, you know, on his speaking tour. I'm surprised his masters let him talk that much. Did you know he was a Marine? And he did CIA training in the 50s.
DENNIS	Why do you have to keep digging up dirt on Doug, Anna? Did it bother you so much that I chose him as my lieutenant that you have to keep rubbing my nose in it?
ANNA	N-no. No! It's just that—well, it's ironic, but if we learned anything from the Doug episode, it's that we do have to tighten up our security, check on people more… it's a shame, because we've always prided ourselves on being accessible to everyone but—
DENNIS	And who's gonna do this checking, Anna? You? Christ, you sound just like him. We gonna hafta do this, check on that…. Well who checks on the people checking?
ANNA	Don't do this, Dennis. This is how we get into trouble.
DENNIS	We are in trouble. *(pause)* Leonard's gonna come in here and ask you a few questions.
ANNA	Leonard is? What kind of questions?
DENNIS	I guess he wants to ask you about what you talked about with the FBI.
ANNA	I *told* you what they wanted. They asked me about the murder of Jeannette Bissonette. But Dennis, you know what it's like. They pick you up, ask you a couple of stupid questions, let you go, and suddenly you're under suspicion because you've been talking to the FBI—
DENNIS	You'll have to talk to Leonard.
ANNA	Why? Why can't I talk to you?
DENNIS	I can't help you. I guess I'm not completely trustworthy either.

She collapses at the table and puts her head down.

ANNA   Fine, send them in. Leonard or whoever. What choice do I have.

> *DENNIS exits. ANNA opens up the letter, reads the poem.*

But the sun is up and you're going?
My heart is filled with tears
Please don't go, I need you walking by my side...
The road is long and weary
And I get so tired...

> *She becomes aware of someone on the other side of the "wall."*

Dennis? Leonard? Leonard?

> *The lights shift and we see a figure with a gun coming through the wall at her.*

Anna Interrogation One By FBI—1975

FBI GUY   Now. Mrs Aquash. You are in the United States of America illegally, and we intend to deport you. You'll be in Canada by this afternoon.

ANNA   I want to see a lawyer.

FBI GUY   Mrs Aquash, you can help us here. Then maybe we can help you. Now I see here that you are charged with possession of a firearm with an obliterated serial number. That's a felony—

ANNA   Really. Well, if I am charged with a felony, I guess I should probably see a lawyer, so—

FBI GUY   You're not going to get a call through until you talk to us first—

ANNA   Who do you guys think you are? I want a lawyer. I'm not talking about anything until there is a lawyer from the Wounded Knee Legal Defence Committee here.

FBI GUY   Mrs Aquash, that's a bit premature. All we want is to ask you a few questions about the events on the Jumping Bull property on June 26th.

ANNA   I don't know anything about it.

FBI GUY   Mrs. Aquash, on June 26th, two FBI agents were murdered in the process of serving a warrant on the Jumping Bull property on the Pine Ridge Reservation. Now we would like you to tell us everything you know about the events of that day.

ANNA   I wasn't there that day. I wish I was, but I wasn't, I was in Cedar Rapids, Iowa, at the Crow Dog trial. I had a speaking engagement there. Sixty people heard me.

FBI GUY   Look, these guys are cold-blooded murderers and we are going to find them, with or without your help.

ANNA   It is so amazing to me that over a hundred Indian people have died violently on Pine Ridge in the last year, but you guys don't give a damn until a couple of

	white FBI's who have no business on reservation land get themselves shot—
FBI GUY	Those agents were friends of mine, Mrs Aquash, who were shot over and over with automatic weapons, stripped and then executed.
ANNA	You guys shouldn't believe your own press. It's gonna get you into trouble someday.
FBI GUY	I have heard that they were scalped.

ANNA begins to laugh her head off.

ANNA	Scalped! Scalped! Oh that's rich! Listen to yourselves! Look Mr FBI Guy, I am almost sorry about your friends, no one deserves to die like that. But have you seen these bullet-riddled bodies of yours? I've seen your papers—saying it was an ambush, saying those agents were shot twenty or thirty times. First of all, those agents had no warrant, they'd been thrown off the property the day before, *so what were they doing there?* Secondly, those men were shot three times, not thirty. *Three times* and—
FBI GUY	That's enough, Mrs Aquash.
ANNA	—and one caught it in the foot and the hand as well as the head, crossfire, returning fire, but no ambush.
FBI GUY	I said that's enough!
ANNA	I know it doesn't really make that much of a difference, obviously three bullets can kill you as good as thirty—
FBI GUY	Will you shut up! Christ you're a mouthy woman!

ANNA is silent.

That's better. Now, Mrs. Aquash, how do you know how many times the agents were shot?

Pause.

ANNA	I know because there was a reporter there by the name of McKiernan. There were witnesses. Look, you can go and get this information yourself, your superiors know,

	they know, it's just easier to keep you guys all revved up—

FBI GUY   Mrs Aquash, do you have children?

Pause.

ANNA   No.

FBI GUY   Mrs Aquash. Do you not have two children, daughters, named Denise and Deborah?

Pause.

Now. Mrs Aquash, where is Leonard Peltier?

ANNA just looks at him.

Where is Leonard Peltier?

ANNA   I don't know.

FBI GUY   Dennis Banks.

She shakes her head.

Mrs Aquash.

She drops her head.

FBI GUY transforms into the LAW.

The Law

LAW	Mrs. Aquash?
	ANNA raises her head and looks at him, discovers herself in court.
	How do you plead? on the two felony charges?
ANNA	N-not guilty.
LAW	Bail is set at $5000.
ANNA	Your honour, may I say something?
LAW	Post haste, Mrs Aquash. Though I warn you, this court is losing patience with this dance between the FBI and AIM.
ANNA	Your honour?
LAW	I resent feeling that this courtroom has become exclusively dedicated to the FBI's pursuit of terrorists in the American Indian Movement. Do you know, Mrs Aquash, I took the unfortunate action of ordering the FBI to turn over its files on AIM, and there were over 315,000 separate file classifications on Wounded Knee alone. It took three vans to deliver them to this court. I was not amused. *(beat)* I am sorry. You wanted to say something.
ANNA	Your Honour, the work I do in Oglala… I am not— none of us are—though the FBI and the media keeps trying to make us out to be terrorists—
LAW	Your point, Mrs Aquash.
ANNA	I am not a terrorist, I am a community worker and I don't understand why I am being punished with the kind of bail that murderers get. What I'm doing on Pine Ridge is working—
LAW	Well Mrs Aquash, if you've been indicted by the grand jury in the matter of the June 26th shootings on Pine Ridge then I'd have to say that this court does not approve of your kind of community work—

ANNA	I'm not indicted in that matter, Your Honour.
LAW	You are not?
ANNA	No, your honour. These are weapons charges—
LAW	Weapons charges?
ANNA	Yes, Your Honour. But my lawyers can't even get the prosecution to turn over the so-called evidence—
LAW	Perhaps they can't find it.
ANNA	Your Honour?
LAW	Well, we are not going forward with this until you have had a fair opportunity to see the evidence. You have rights under the law, Mrs Aquash.
ANNA	(*beat*) Yes—
	LAW stops and seems to smell the air.
LAW	I assume you are able to post 10% of the $5000. You are free to go until the prosecution sees fit to share its evidence with your lawyers. If they do not, and I would not be at all surprised if they did not, I will dismiss this case on the grounds of government misconduct.
ANNA	I am free to go?
LAW	Indeed. Mrs. Aquash. I am sorry about Wounded Knee. The first one.
ANNA	(*beat*) Thank you, Your Honour.
	He exits. ANNA moves to the phone booth.

Phone Call One

Through this, we feel the RUGARU's presence on the other side of the wall, smelling her, hunting her.

ANNA   Hi sweetie, it's mommy. How are you? Good, good. And your sister? That's good, chickadee, you've got to take care of Deborah. Because you're older, that's why. Oh you got it? Good, that was fast. Yeah, *(touching hair)* I know it's long, I haven't cut it in a long time. It's even longer now than in that picture. *(beat)* I can't come home right now, Denise, but I'm always with you, with you and your sister—that's right sweetie, like a guardian angel.

Is Deborah there sweetie? No, no, don't wake her up. Just tell her—just tell her I called… I gotta go now sweetie. Bye now. Bye bye.

The Deal

She steps out of the phone booth and FBI GUY steps out from behind the booth and handcuffs her. He throws her into a chair.

He holds a letter in front of her face.

FBI GUY   Here's the deal Anna Mae. You testify against Darelle "Dino" Butler and Nilak Butler at the grand jury, we'll drop one felony charge. Your lawyer even says it's a good deal. See?

ANNA   Dino and Nilak didn't do anything.

FBI GUY   We're going to get them with or without you.

ANNA   No.

FBI GUY   This is a one-time offer only, girlie. You'd be wise to take it.

ANNA   No.

FBI GUY   Fine. It's your funeral.

ANNA   I know.

FBI GUY   Right then. You're free to go.

ANNA   *(puzzled)* I am?

The handcuffs come off in her hands.

FBI GUY   Stay out of trouble.

He takes the cuffs and exits.

ANNA   Ha. All the fingerprints you guys took, I'd have to cut my hands off to get away with anything.

Phone Call Two

ANNA goes back to the phone, dials. Again we feel
the presence behind the wall, this time he is pushing
at her, she leans against him, then senses it's not just
a phone booth.

ANNA   Rebecca, better speak in Micmac… wiretaps. Listen—
I've been in jail, it's not going to stop now. Home?
I—can't come home. I'm way too deep in it now…
I *wasn't* there, I wish I was…. Because if I'd *been* there,
then maybe things would've turned out differently.

These woods are full of men, they're out to get me…
they'll kill me if the FBI doesn't get me. I can't Becky,
I gotta go. Kiss the girls for me, 'kay?

She collapses in the phone booth, weeping. The arms
of the creature behind the wall come through the
wall, wrapping themselves around her. She scrambles
away from them.

Interrogation Two

Lights change and she is isolated in a light. The interrogator is unseen.

ANNA   Look, here's what I know. The day before the shootings—*the day before*—the so-called tribal chairman of Pine Ridge, Dick Wilson, that bastard, transferred the title of one-eighth of the reservation to the government. Transferred in secret. Don't you think that's a little too convenient? That they've got us all tied up with raids and warrants and guns and court dates, and all the while Dickie's in the back room selling out his people?

LAWRENCE   We all know Wilson's crooked, Anna Mae, but what would the government want with that piece of land? It's dry and ugly, nothing will grow on it.

ANNA   I think there's something in the earth there, something they want. What if it's uranium? That makes sense, doesn't it? The miscarriages, the birth defects. They're pulling something out of the earth that's poisoning us—

LAWRENCE   There's no proof. So far all we've got is your allegation that Dickie transferred part of the reserve to the government—

ANNA   Proof is easy. All we have to do is get our hands on some water samples, have them checked out, I bet we find high levels of something, probably uranium—

LAWRENCE   Where'd you get this information, Anna Mae?

ANNA   Lawrence? It is you, isn't it? Lawrence, look, can we just talk like human beings?

LAWRENCE   Answer the question, Anna Mae.

ANNA   I have answered the question. I have answered all the questions! You guys are acting just like them—

LAWRENCE   Where did you get this information, Anna Mae?

ANNA	I told you! It's a matter of public record! If we weren't so busy running around with our little guns and our big paranoias, and paid more attention to the ways we're being screwed—
LAWRENCE	Where'd you get this information, Anna? Why now? Right after you've been released by the pigs?
ANNA	What has happened to you, Lawrence? Is this what you've learned in the service of the Movement? Does it make you proud?
LAWRENCE	What did you talk about with the FBI?
ANNA	Is the revolution what your Rugaru foretold? That our men would be interrogating our women on their knees?
LAWRENCE	What did you talk about with the FBI?
ANNA	I told you. I told you already.
LAWRENCE	Tell me again.

Phone Call Three

ANNA
—it's all gone to hell—I think they let me go thinking I would lead them to Leonard and Dennis, and now everyone thinks that I'm an informer—

The RUGARU appears to ANNA.

I'm—thanks—but I'm going to spend Christmas with some friends on Pine Ridge, it'll be safer…. No, it'll be fine, I'll just make sure I'm always with a group of the women, no one would dare touch me. I should be in Minneapolis by January. I've got some really interesting information—

The RUGARU moves in on her. She moves towards him. Stopped by the phone cord. He lowers his head to her neck and smells. Lick? Nip?

Not on the phone. It's not safe. I'll see you in Minneapolis.

She drops the phone. The RUGARU exits and she is left CS.

End

I started survival schools in the States. The idea was, if we could give kids the tools to live in the white world, but not let them lose their Indian-ness, give 'em a sense of pride in who they were, where they come from, we could help to rebuild an Indian Nation that was self-sufficient, autonomous, healthy and whole.

I started survival schools. Those who can, do. Those who can't, teach. Those who can't, can't. Don't. Don't.

The man has entered and is watching her, smelling her. He is man, with elements of LAWRENCE, DENNIS, FBI GUY, but he moves like an animal. She becomes aware of him.

As he approaches her, her "don'ts" become more agitated, pleading, angry, anguished. As he rapes her, she stops begging and begins to say:

My name is Anna Mae Pictou Aquash, Micmac Nation from Shubenacadie, Nova Scotia. My mother is Mary Ellen Pictou, my father is Francis Thomas Levi, my sisters are Rebecca Julien and Mary Lafford, my brother is Francis. My daughters are Denise and Deborah. You cannot kill us all. You can kill me, but my sisters live, my daughters live. You cannot kill us all. My sisters live. Becky and Mary, Helen and Priscilla, Janet and Raven, Sylvia, Ellen, Pelajia, Agnes, Monica, Edie, Jessica, Gloria and Lisa and Muriel, Monique, Joy and Tina, Margo, Maria, Beatrice, Minnie, April, Colleen, Kimi, Michelle...

You can kill me, but you cannot kill us all. You can kill me.

There is a gunshot. She falls, curls into a foetal position, the good red road emanating from her. Blackout.

The end.

Yvette Nolan is a playwright, dramaturg, and director. In 1996, she was the Aboriginal Writer in Residence at Brandon University, where she wrote the first draft of *Annie Mae's Movement*. Her other plays include *BLADE*, *Job's Wife*, *Video*, the libretto *Hilda Blake* and the radio play *Owen*. She is also the editor of *Beyond the Pale: Dramatic Writing from First Nations Writers and Writers of Colour*. She was the president of Playwrights Union of Canada from 1998–2001, and of Playwrights Canada Press from 2003–2005. Born in Prince Albert, Saskatchewan to an Algonquin mother and an Irish immigrant father, raised in Winnipeg, Manitoba, she lived in the Yukon and Nova Scotia before moving to Toronto to take the helm at Native Earth Performing Arts.